# SOCCER SUE

By Jane Vecchio

Illustrated by Molly Delaney

Modern Curriculum Press

**Credits**

**Illustrations:** Molly Delaney

Computer colorizations by Lucie Maragni

Cover and book design by Lisa Ann Arcuri

ISBN 0-7652-1370-2

Printed in the United States of America

6 7 8 9 10 11    07 06 05 04

**1-800-321-3106**
**www.pearsonlearning.com**

# Contents

**For Mark,
who showed me how to have
fun in sports and in life!**

# Chapter 1
# A New Sport

"Look, Sue. The soccer team meeting is this week!" Rita pointed to the paper on the bulletin board outside their classroom. The paper said, "Do you like to play soccer? Come join the Tigers soccer team on Friday. Meet at 3:00 in the gym."

"Your sister plays soccer," Rita said to Sue. "She is always talking about how much fun it is. Let's join the team."

"It does sound like fun," Sue said. "I don't know anything about soccer."

"We can learn. Come on. Let's go," Rita said.

"Well, all right," Sue said.

That Friday after school, Rita and Sue went to the gym. A lot of people were there. Everyone talked at once. Then a man with a nice smile began to talk. The room became quiet.

"Hi," the man said. "I'm Coach Lopez, the soccer coach. How many of you have played soccer before?" he asked.

A few hands went up. "Well, more people like soccer than any other sport in the world!" he said.

"More than baseball?" someone asked.

"Yes," Coach Lopez said. "It's a ball game that is played mostly with the feet."

Sue and Rita wiggled their feet.

Coach Lopez gave everyone a T-shirt. The shirts had the word TIGERS printed on the front.

"This is your team shirt," he said.

Sue put her shirt on over her sweater.

"How do I look?" she asked Rita.

"Lumpy," Rita said. They both laughed.

Coach Lopez held up two long pads. "You will get these special pads to put on your legs," he said. "They are shin guards. You wear them under long socks. They keep your legs from getting hurt if the ball hits them."

"You will also need special shoes that have bumps on the bottom," Coach Lopez said. "The bumps are called cleats. They help to keep you from sliding in the grass."

Coach Lopez passed out a list of games and practice times. "I'll see you all tomorrow for our first practice!" he said.

# Chapter 2
# On the Field

The next day was bright and sunny. Rita and Sue got to the soccer field early.

"Okay, Tigers, line up!" said Coach Lopez. "I'll show you how to kick the ball."

The kids lined up. Coach Lopez showed them how to point their toes down. Then he had them practice bending their knees and kicking out. "Kick the ball on the laces of your shoes, not with the toes," he said.

Everyone chose a partner. First Sue rolled the ball to Rita. She kicked it back.

Then it was Sue's turn. Rita rolled the ball. Sue made sure to keep her toes down. Then she kicked hard. Her foot missed the ball. She landed on the grass.

"Oops!" said Sue.

Next Coach Lopez showed the Tigers how to stop the ball. Players kicked the ball toward him. He did not touch it with his hands. He let the ball bounce off his shoulders. Then it bounced off his arms and then his legs. When it was Sue's turn to stop the ball, she caught it!

"In soccer you can't use your hands. It's a rule," Coach Lopez said.

"I can't use my hands?" Sue cried. "What kind of a ball game is this?"

The rest of the practice was hard for Sue. She caught her toes in the grass trying to kick the ball. She kept catching the ball in her hands. She heard someone say, "Sue's not doing very well." She felt like crying.

At the end of the practice, Coach Lopez said to the players, "You're doing fine. On our team we support and help each other. Do all you Tigers understand?"

"Yes!" said the kids.

"I'm not a very good soccer player," Sue thought. "Maybe I'll quit."

# Chapter 3
# Will Sue Quit?

When Sue got home, her older sister was there. "How was soccer?" Annie asked.

Sue said, "Soccer is hard. I think I'll quit."

Annie said, "Don't give up yet. It takes time and practice. Just relax and have fun."

Sue was quiet. She liked the Tigers. She liked Coach Lopez. She did like soccer even if it was hard. She wanted to play!

The next afternoon, Annie said, "Let's go outside. I'll help you practice."

Annie started to move the ball around the yard with her feet. Sue couldn't believe how fast her sister's feet were moving.

"I'll kick the ball to you," called Annie. "Kick it back."

Annie kicked the ball. Sue almost missed it. Then she turned and kicked it back.

"You're getting it," Annie said. "Now try stopping the ball."

Annie kicked the ball. The ball hit the house. It popped back up. Sue caught it.

"Put your hands in your pockets. Then you can't catch the ball," Annie said.

Sue shoved her hands in her pockets. Then she kicked the ball against the side of the house. The ball popped up. Sue turned. The ball bounced off her arm.

"That's it!" Annie cheered.

Just then Sue and Annie's father came
outside. "What's all the noise?" he asked.

"I'm helping Sue practice," Annie said. She
kicked the ball at Sue. Sue kicked it back.

"Hey, that's great," their dad said.

Sue thought, "I'm doing well now. What
will happen when I play with the Tigers?"

# Chapter 4
# Tiger Teamwork

As the days went by, Sue practiced hard. She was a good kicker and a good runner. She still could not stop catching the ball sometimes.

"I think my hands have soccer ball glue on them!" Sue said.

"Don't give up," said Coach Lopez.

Little by little the Tigers learned to run
and kick the ball at the same time. Coach
Lopez called this "dribbling" the ball.

"Is dribbling like this?" asked Jeremy. He
took a drink from his water bottle. The water
spilled down his chin. Jeremy and the Tigers
laughed.

26

The Tigers also learned how to score or make points. Coach Lopez pointed to the nets at each end of the field. "Those nets are the goals," he said. "Kick the ball into the other team's net. Then you make a point."

Coach Lopez chose Rita to be the goalie. The goalie had to keep the ball out of the net. Only the goalie could catch and throw the ball.

Another few days went by. At last it was time for the Tigers to play their first game. Sue was scared. What if she fell on the ground? Anything could happen!

When the game started, Sue tried to remember everything she had learned. Once the ball hit her in the leg. She was really glad she had her shin guards on.

The Tigers played better as the game went on. They dribbled the ball. Rita stopped balls from going into the Tigers' goal. Sue kicked the ball. When it came toward her she caught it six times in a row!

Week after week the Tigers played. Sue
tried hard not to catch the ball. She even put
her hands in her pockets. Then someone ran
into her and knocked her down.

"Will I ever feel like a real Tiger?" she
thought. Every day she wanted to quit. Rita
or Annie talked her out of it.

# Chapter 5
# No Goalie!

The Tigers were doing well, but they had to win the next game. Then they would have a chance to win the championship. They had one more practice before the big game.

Coach Lopez had the players practice
moving the ball down the field toward the
goal. Jeremy dribbled the ball to the net.
Then he kicked it hard. Rita jumped to stop
the ball. When she landed, she fell.

"Ow, my ankle!" she cried. Everyone
rushed to help her.

"Rita, I think you've twisted your ankle," said Coach Lopez.

"What are we going to do?" asked Tara. "Now we don't have a goalie."

The Tigers looked at each other. Then, one by one, the Tigers turned and looked at Sue.

"Sue is really good at catching the ball!" said Keisha.

"She is not afraid of falling," said Max.

"Sue should be our goalie!" yelled the Tigers.

"Good idea," said Coach Lopez.

Sue took her place in front of the net. The other Tigers tried to kick the ball past her. The ball was fast. Sue had always tried to keep her hands away from the ball. Now she had to catch it.

When Sue got home she told her mom about being the goalie for the big game. Then Sue called Rita on the phone.

"I'm sorry you hurt your ankle," said Sue.

"Thanks, Sue," Rita said. "It will be all right. You'll be a great goalie."

Sue went outside to practice. SLAM!
SLAM! went the ball against the side of
Sue's house. Now Sue had to practice
keeping her hands OUT of her pockets.

Annie came outside to watch Sue practice. "What are you doing?" she asked. "Why are you catching the ball?"

"I'm the new goalie," said Sue. "Now I'm supposed to catch the ball."

"Wow!" Annie said. "I bet you'll be a great goalie!" Sue wasn't so sure.

# Chapter 6
# The Big Game

It was the day of the big game with the Bees. Sue stood in front of the Tigers' goal. She felt her knees shake. She was nervous.

Sue saw her family. Rita was there, too. They waved and smiled.

The Bees ran onto the field. They had
yellow and black T-shirts. They really looked
like big bees. Sue laughed. She felt a little bit
better.

The game began. Right away the Bees dribbled the ball to the Tigers' goal. A Bee kicked the ball up into the air. It flew past Sue's head and went into the net! The Bees scored one goal.

"Oh, no," Sue groaned. "I will stop the next ball. Hands, stay out of my pockets!"

She was ready the next time the ball came toward her. A Bee kicked the ball. Sue jumped high and caught it! She tossed it back into the game. She smiled.

The game went on and on. Sue caught the ball many times. She fell on the ground. She bumped the ball away with her feet and shoulders. She forgot all about wanting to quit the team. She just played her very best.

There were only three minutes left in the game. The scoreboard showed that the Tigers were ahead. They had five goals. The Bees had four goals.

The Bees got the ball. They ran with it right toward Sue in the Tigers' goal.

Sue got ready. The Bees kicked the ball. She jumped. She felt her hands close around the ball. She caught it! The ball did not go in the net.

Sue had stopped the Bees from scoring the goal that would have tied the game. Now the game was over. The Tigers had won!

Sue heard her family yelling, "Hooray!"
She saw Coach Lopez and all the Tigers
running toward her. The players all yelled,
"Yeah for Soccer Sue! Yeah for Soccer Sue!"

Sue remembered how she had wanted to give up. She also remembered how upset she had been when she could not stop catching the ball. Then Sue remembered all her hard work. She smiled. Soccer Sue knew she was a real Tiger at last.

# Glossary

**coach**   [kohch]  person who teaches or trains people in a sport

**guard**   [gahrd]  protect

**gym**   [jihm]  large room where people can exercise and play sports

**nervous**   [NUR vus]  scared and worried

**quit**   [kwiht]  to leave or to stop doing something

**relax**   [ree LAKS]  to loosen up, to calm down

**shin**   [shihn]  long bone in your leg below your knee

**support**   [suyh PORT]  to help, to be on someone's side